How to be prepare for a rush?

For a Fast Food Restaurant

Ruby Martos

For information, contact

Ruby Martos

rubyms@nmsu.edu

Dedication

To my mom and family that are my inspiration to keep going and be better everyday.

How to use this workbook

Please fill out the information needed and write manager's initial in each box as you get prepare for the rush.

Rush ready

Day Manager:_____ Night Manager:_____

Mgr Initials

People	AM	PM
Staff properly deployed. Everyone knows primary and secondary position		
Drive thru service ambassadors only pull cars up if the car behind has food ready		
Opening manager communicates any special events expected		
Equipment	**AM**	**PM**
3 headsets in use and back up batteries charged		
All heating equipment working properly		
Cash drawers stocked with change/ Printers stocked with paper		
Condiments, paper goods, and utensils are stocked for projected sales volume in appropriate areas		
Lobby tables, floors, trash receptacles, windows , bathrooms, and condiment stand are clean, stocked and ready for guest use		
All trash cans have been emptied and cleaned appropriately		
All kitchen floors and equipment are cleaned		
All dishes, utensils, and portioning equipment is washed, sanitized, air dried and positioned at work stations		
Fryers have been filtered and/or warm soaked and tested		

Products	Mgr Initials	
	PM	AM
Manager on duty completes and owns production guide		
Holding cabinet's temperature set as appropriate		
Low boy freezer stocked		
Drive thru area organized with all condiments		
Packing supplies and condiments stocked		
Production Charts are printed and posted		
Hot held products are available, prepped, portioned, and labeled with holding times		
Frozen ready-to-cook items are stocked and stored in the kitchen or cooks line freezer units for prompt accessibility		
Pre-cook products are in steam wells ready for portioning		

Comments

_____

_____

_____

_____

_____

_____

_____

_____

_____

_____

Rush ready

Day Manager:_____ Night Manager:_____

People	AM	PM
Staff properly deployed. Everyone knows primary and secondary position		
Drive thru service ambassadors only pull cars up if the car behind has food ready		
Opening manager communicates any special events expected		

Equipment	AM	PM
3 headsets in use and back up batteries charged		
All heating equipment working properly		
Cash drawers stocked with change/ Printers stocked with paper		
Condiments, paper goods, and utensils are stocked for projected sales volume in appropriate areas		
Lobby tables, floors, trash receptacles, windows , bathrooms, and condiment stand are clean, stocked and ready for guest use		
All trash cans have been emptied and cleaned appropriately		
All kitchen floors and equipment are cleaned		
All dishes, utensils, and portioning equipment is washed, sanitized, air dried and positioned at work stations		
Fryers have been filtered and/or warm soaked and tested		

	Mgr Initials	
Products	**PM**	**AM**
Manager on duty completes and owns production guide		
Holding cabinet's temperature set as appropriate		
Low boy freezer stocked		
Drive thru area organized with all condiments		
Packing supplies and condiments stocked		
Production Charts are printed and posted		
Hot held products are available, prepped, portioned, and labeled with holding times		
Frozen ready-to-cook items are stocked and stored in the kitchen or cooks line freezer units for prompt accessibility		
Pre-cook products are in steam wells ready for portioning		

Comments

_____
_____
_____
_____
_____
_____
_____
_____
_____
_____

Rush ready

Day Manager:_____ Night Manager:_____

Mgr Initials

People	AM	PM
Staff properly deployed. Everyone knows primary and secondary position		
Drive thru service ambassadors only pull cars up if the car behind has food ready		
Opening manager communicates any special events expected		
Equipment	**AM**	**PM**
3 headsets in use and back up batteries charged		
All heating equipment working properly		
Cash drawers stocked with change/ Printers stocked with paper		
Condiments, paper goods, and utensils are stocked for projected sales volume in appropriate areas		
Lobby tables, floors, trash receptacles, windows , bathrooms, and condiment stand are clean, stocked and ready for guest use		
All trash cans have been emptied and cleaned appropriately		
All kitchen floors and equipment are cleaned		
All dishes, utensils, and portioning equipment is washed, sanitized, air dried and positioned at work stations		
Fryers have been filtered and/or warm soaked and tested		

Products	Mgr Initials	
	PM	AM
Manager on duty completes and owns production guide		
Holding cabinet's temperature set as appropriate		
Low boy freezer stocked		
Drive thru area organized with all condiments		
Packing supplies and condiments stocked		
Production Charts are printed and posted		
Hot held products are available, prepped, portioned, and labeled with holding times		
Frozen ready-to-cook items are stocked and stored in the kitchen or cooks line freezer units for prompt accessibility		
Pre-cook products are in steam wells ready for portioning		

Comments

_____
_____
_____
_____
_____
_____
_____
_____
_____
_____

Rush ready

Day Manager:_____ Night Manager:_____

Mgr Initials

People	AM	PM
Staff properly deployed. Everyone knows primary and secondary position		
Drive thru service ambassadors only pull cars up if the car behind has food ready		
Opening manager communicates any special events expected		

Equipment	AM	PM
3 headsets in use and back up batteries charged		
All heating equipment working properly		
Cash drawers stocked with change/ Printers stocked with paper		
Condiments, paper goods, and utensils are stocked for projected sales volume in appropriate areas		
Lobby tables, floors, trash receptacles, windows , bathrooms, and condiment stand are clean, stocked and ready for guest use		
All trash cans have been emptied and cleaned appropriately		
All kitchen floors and equipment are cleaned		
All dishes, utensils, and portioning equipment is washed, sanitized, air dried and positioned at work stations		
Fryers have been filtered and/or warm soaked and tested		

Products	Mgr Initials	
	PM	AM
Manager on duty completes and owns production guide		
Holding cabinet's temperature set as appropriate		
Low boy freezer stocked		
Drive thru area organized with all condiments		
Packing supplies and condiments stocked		
Production Charts are printed and posted		
Hot held products are available, prepped, portioned, and labeled with holding times		
Frozen ready-to-cook items are stocked and stored in the kitchen or cooks line freezer units for prompt accessibility		
Pre-cook products are in steam wells ready for portioning		

Comments

Rush ready

Day Manager:_____ Night Manager:_____

	Mgr Initials	
People	**AM**	**PM**
Staff properly deployed. Everyone knows primary and secondary position		
Drive thru service ambassadors only pull cars up if the car behind has food ready		
Opening manager communicates any special events expected		
Equipment	**AM**	**PM**
3 headsets in use and back up batteries charged		
All heating equipment working properly		
Cash drawers stocked with change/ Printers stocked with paper		
Condiments, paper goods, and utensils are stocked for projected sales volume in appropriate areas		
Lobby tables, floors, trash receptacles, windows , bathrooms, and condiment stand are clean, stocked and ready for guest use		
All trash cans have been emptied and cleaned appropriately		
All kitchen floors and equipment are cleaned		
All dishes, utensils, and portioning equipment is washed, sanitized, air dried and positioned at work stations		
Fryers have been filtered and/or warm soaked and tested		

Products	Mgr Initials	
	PM	AM
Manager on duty completes and owns production guide		
Holding cabinet's temperature set as appropriate		
Low boy freezer stocked		
Drive thru area organized with all condiments		
Packing supplies and condiments stocked		
Production Charts are printed and posted		
Hot held products are available, prepped, portioned, and labeled with holding times		
Frozen ready-to-cook items are stocked and stored in the kitchen or cooks line freezer units for prompt accessibility		
Pre-cook products are in steam wells ready for portioning		

Comments

_____
_____
_____
_____
_____
_____
_____
_____
_____

Rush ready

Day Manager:_____ Night Manager:_____

Mgr Initials

People	AM	PM
Staff properly deployed. Everyone knows primary and secondary position		
Drive thru service ambassadors only pull cars up if the car behind has food ready		
Opening manager communicates any special events expected		
Equipment	**AM**	**PM**
3 headsets in use and back up batteries charged		
All heating equipment working properly		
Cash drawers stocked with change/ Printers stocked with paper		
Condiments, paper goods, and utensils are stocked for projected sales volume in appropriate areas		
Lobby tables, floors, trash receptacles, windows , bathrooms, and condiment stand are clean, stocked and ready for guest use		
All trash cans have been emptied and cleaned appropriately		
All kitchen floors and equipment are cleaned		
All dishes, utensils, and portioning equipment is washed, sanitized, air dried and positioned at work stations		
Fryers have been filtered and/or warm soaked and tested		

Products	Mgr Initials	
	PM	AM
Manager on duty completes and owns production guide		
Holding cabinet's temperature set as appropriate		
Low boy freezer stocked		
Drive thru area organized with all condiments		
Packing supplies and condiments stocked		
Production Charts are printed and posted		
Hot held products are available, prepped, portioned, and labeled with holding times		
Frozen ready-to-cook items are stocked and stored in the kitchen or cooks line freezer units for prompt accessibility		
Pre-cook products are in steam wells ready for portioning		

Comments

_____

_____

_____

_____

_____

_____

_____

_____

_____

Rush ready

Day Manager:_____ Night Manager:_____

Mgr Initials

People	AM	PM
Staff properly deployed. Everyone knows primary and secondary position		
Drive thru service ambassadors only pull cars up if the car behind has food ready		
Opening manager communicates any special events expected		
Equipment	**AM**	**PM**
3 headsets in use and back up batteries charged		
All heating equipment working properly		
Cash drawers stocked with change/ Printers stocked with paper		
Condiments, paper goods, and utensils are stocked for projected sales volume in appropriate areas		
Lobby tables, floors, trash receptacles, windows , bathrooms, and condiment stand are clean, stocked and ready for guest use		
All trash cans have been emptied and cleaned appropriately		
All kitchen floors and equipment are cleaned		
All dishes, utensils, and portioning equipment is washed, sanitized, air dried and positioned at work stations		
Fryers have been filtered and/or warm soaked and tested		

	Mgr Initials	
Products	**PM**	**AM**
Manager on duty completes and owns production guide		
Holding cabinet's temperature set as appropriate		
Low boy freezer stocked		
Drive thru area organized with all condiments		
Packing supplies and condiments stocked		
Production Charts are printed and posted		
Hot held products are available, prepped, portioned, and labeled with holding times		
Frozen ready-to-cook items are stocked and stored in the kitchen or cooks line freezer units for prompt accessibility		
Pre-cook products are in steam wells ready for portioning		

Comments

_____

_____

_____

_____

_____

_____

_____

_____

_____

Rush ready

Day Manager:_____ Night Manager:_____

People	AM	PM
Staff properly deployed. Everyone knows primary and secondary position		
Drive thru service ambassadors only pull cars up if the car behind has food ready		
Opening manager communicates any special events expected		

Equipment	AM	PM
3 headsets in use and back up batteries charged		
All heating equipment working properly		
Cash drawers stocked with change/ Printers stocked with paper		
Condiments, paper goods, and utensils are stocked for projected sales volume in appropriate areas		
Lobby tables, floors, trash receptacles, windows , bathrooms, and condiment stand are clean, stocked and ready for guest use		
All trash cans have been emptied and cleaned appropriately		
All kitchen floors and equipment are cleaned		
All dishes, utensils, and portioning equipment is washed, sanitized, air dried and positioned at work stations		
Fryers have been filtered and/or warm soaked and tested		

Products	Mgr Initials	
	PM	AM
Manager on duty completes and owns production guide		
Holding cabinet's temperature set as appropriate		
Low boy freezer stocked		
Drive thru area organized with all condiments		
Packing supplies and condiments stocked		
Production Charts are printed and posted		
Hot held products are available, prepped, portioned, and labeled with holding times		
Frozen ready-to-cook items are stocked and stored in the kitchen or cooks line freezer units for prompt accessibility		
Pre-cook products are in steam wells ready for portioning		

Comments

_____

_____

_____

_____

_____

_____

_____

_____

_____

_____

Rush ready

Day Manager:_____   Night Manager:_____

Mgr Initials

People	AM	PM
Staff properly deployed. Everyone knows primary and secondary position		
Drive thru service ambassadors only pull cars up if the car behind has food ready		
Opening manager communicates any special events expected		

Equipment	AM	PM
3 headsets in use and back up batteries charged		
All heating equipment working properly		
Cash drawers stocked with change/ Printers stocked with paper		
Condiments, paper goods, and utensils are stocked for projected sales volume in appropriate areas		
Lobby tables, floors, trash receptacles, windows , bathrooms, and condiment stand are clean, stocked and ready for guest use		
All trash cans have been emptied and cleaned appropriately		
All kitchen floors and equipment are cleaned		
All dishes, utensils, and portioning equipment is washed, sanitized, air dried and positioned at work stations		
Fryers have been filtered and/or warm soaked and tested		

Mgr Initials

Products	PM	AM
Manager on duty completes and owns production guide		
Holding cabinet's temperature set as appropriate		
Low boy freezer stocked		
Drive thru area organized with all condiments		
Packing supplies and condiments stocked		
Production Charts are printed and posted		
Hot held products are available, prepped, portioned, and labeled with holding times		
Frozen ready-to-cook items are stocked and stored in the kitchen or cooks line freezer units for prompt accessibility		
Pre-cook products are in steam wells ready for portioning		

Comments

_____
_____
_____
_____
_____
_____
_____
_____
_____
_____

Rush ready

Day Manager:_____ Night Manager:_____

Mgr Initials

People	AM	PM
Staff properly deployed. Everyone knows primary and secondary position		
Drive thru service ambassadors only pull cars up if the car behind has food ready		
Opening manager communicates any special events expected		
Equipment	**AM**	**PM**
3 headsets in use and back up batteries charged		
All heating equipment working properly		
Cash drawers stocked with change/ Printers stocked with paper		
Condiments, paper goods, and utensils are stocked for projected sales volume in appropriate areas		
Lobby tables, floors, trash receptacles, windows , bathrooms, and condiment stand are clean, stocked and ready for guest use		
All trash cans have been emptied and cleaned appropriately		
All kitchen floors and equipment are cleaned		
All dishes, utensils, and portioning equipment is washed, sanitized, air dried and positioned at work stations		
Fryers have been filtered and/or warm soaked and tested		

| | Mgr Initials | |
Products	PM	AM
Manager on duty completes and owns production guide		
Holding cabinet's temperature set as appropriate		
Low boy freezer stocked		
Drive thru area organized with all condiments		
Packing supplies and condiments stocked		
Production Charts are printed and posted		
Hot held products are available, prepped, portioned, and labeled with holding times		
Frozen ready-to-cook items are stocked and stored in the kitchen or cooks line freezer units for prompt accessibility		
Pre-cook products are in steam wells ready for portioning		

Comments

_____

_____

_____

_____

_____

_____

_____

_____

_____

Rush ready

Day Manager:_____ Night Manager:_____

People	AM	PM
Staff properly deployed. Everyone knows primary and secondary position		
Drive thru service ambassadors only pull cars up if the car behind has food ready		
Opening manager communicates any special events expected		
Equipment	**AM**	**PM**
3 headsets in use and back up batteries charged		
All heating equipment working properly		
Cash drawers stocked with change/ Printers stocked with paper		
Condiments, paper goods, and utensils are stocked for projected sales volume in appropriate areas		
Lobby tables, floors, trash receptacles, windows , bathrooms, and condiment stand are clean, stocked and ready for guest use		
All trash cans have been emptied and cleaned appropriately		
All kitchen floors and equipment are cleaned		
All dishes, utensils, and portioning equipment is washed, sanitized, air dried and positioned at work stations		
Fryers have been filtered and/or warm soaked and tested		

Products	Mgr Initials	
	PM	AM
Manager on duty completes and owns production guide		
Holding cabinet's temperature set as appropriate		
Low boy freezer stocked		
Drive thru area organized with all condiments		
Packing supplies and condiments stocked		
Production Charts are printed and posted		
Hot held products are available, prepped, portioned, and labeled with holding times		
Frozen ready-to-cook items are stocked and stored in the kitchen or cooks line freezer units for prompt accessibility		
Pre-cook products are in steam wells ready for portioning		

Comments

_____
_____
_____
_____
_____
_____
_____
_____
_____
_____
_____

Rush ready

Day Manager:_____   Night Manager:_____

Mgr Initials

People	AM	PM
Staff properly deployed. Everyone knows primary and secondary position		
Drive thru service ambassadors only pull cars up if the car behind has food ready		
Opening manager communicates any special events expected		

Equipment	AM	PM
3 headsets in use and back up batteries charged		
All heating equipment working properly		
Cash drawers stocked with change/ Printers stocked with paper		
Condiments, paper goods, and utensils are stocked for projected sales volume in appropriate areas		
Lobby tables, floors, trash receptacles, windows , bathrooms, and condiment stand are clean, stocked and ready for guest use		
All trash cans have been emptied and cleaned appropriately		
All kitchen floors and equipment are cleaned		
All dishes, utensils, and portioning equipment is washed, sanitized, air dried and positioned at work stations		
Fryers have been filtered and/or warm soaked and tested		

Products	Mgr Initials	
	PM	AM
Manager on duty completes and owns production guide		
Holding cabinet's temperature set as appropriate		
Low boy freezer stocked		
Drive thru area organized with all condiments		
Packing supplies and condiments stocked		
Production Charts are printed and posted		
Hot held products are available, prepped, portioned, and labeled with holding times		
Frozen ready-to-cook items are stocked and stored in the kitchen or cooks line freezer units for prompt accessibility		
Pre-cook products are in steam wells ready for portioning		

Comments

_____

_____

_____

_____

_____

_____

_____

_____

_____

_____

Rush ready

Day Manager:_____ Night Manager:_____

People	AM	PM
Staff properly deployed. Everyone knows primary and secondary position		
Drive thru service ambassadors only pull cars up if the car behind has food ready		
Opening manager communicates any special events expected		
Equipment	**AM**	**PM**
3 headsets in use and back up batteries charged		
All heating equipment working properly		
Cash drawers stocked with change/ Printers stocked with paper		
Condiments, paper goods, and utensils are stocked for projected sales volume in appropriate areas		
Lobby tables, floors, trash receptacles, windows , bathrooms, and condiment stand are clean, stocked and ready for guest use		
All trash cans have been emptied and cleaned appropriately		
All kitchen floors and equipment are cleaned		
All dishes, utensils, and portioning equipment is washed, sanitized, air dried and positioned at work stations		
Fryers have been filtered and/or warm soaked and tested		

Products	Mgr Initials	
	PM	AM
Manager on duty completes and owns production guide		
Holding cabinet's temperature set as appropriate		
Low boy freezer stocked		
Drive thru area organized with all condiments		
Packing supplies and condiments stocked		
Production Charts are printed and posted		
Hot held products are available, prepped, portioned, and labeled with holding times		
Frozen ready-to-cook items are stocked and stored in the kitchen or cooks line freezer units for prompt accessibility		
Pre-cook products are in steam wells ready for portioning		

Comments

_____

_____

_____

_____

_____

_____

_____

_____

_____

_____

Rush ready

Day Manager:_____   Night Manager:_____

People	AM	PM
Staff properly deployed. Everyone knows primary and secondary position		
Drive thru service ambassadors only pull cars up if the car behind has food ready		
Opening manager communicates any special events expected		

Equipment	AM	PM
3 headsets in use and back up batteries charged		
All heating equipment working properly		
Cash drawers stocked with change/ Printers stocked with paper		
Condiments, paper goods, and utensils are stocked for projected sales volume in appropriate areas		
Lobby tables, floors, trash receptacles, windows , bathrooms, and condiment stand are clean, stocked and ready for guest use		
All trash cans have been emptied and cleaned appropriately		
All kitchen floors and equipment are cleaned		
All dishes, utensils, and portioning equipment is washed, sanitized, air dried and positioned at work stations		
Fryers have been filtered and/or warm soaked and tested		

Products	Mgr Initials	
	PM	AM
Manager on duty completes and owns production guide		
Holding cabinet's temperature set as appropriate		
Low boy freezer stocked		
Drive thru area organized with all condiments		
Packing supplies and condiments stocked		
Production Charts are printed and posted		
Hot held products are available, prepped, portioned, and labeled with holding times		
Frozen ready-to-cook items are stocked and stored in the kitchen or cooks line freezer units for prompt accessibility		
Pre-cook products are in steam wells ready for portioning		

Comments

_____

_____

_____

_____

_____

_____

_____

_____

_____

_____

Rush ready

Day Manager:_____ Night Manager:_____

Mgr Initials

People	AM	PM
Staff properly deployed. Everyone knows primary and secondary position		
Drive thru service ambassadors only pull cars up if the car behind has food ready		
Opening manager communicates any special events expected		

Equipment	AM	PM
3 headsets in use and back up batteries charged		
All heating equipment working properly		
Cash drawers stocked with change/ Printers stocked with paper		
Condiments, paper goods, and utensils are stocked for projected sales volume in appropriate areas		
Lobby tables, floors, trash receptacles, windows , bathrooms, and condiment stand are clean, stocked and ready for guest use		
All trash cans have been emptied and cleaned appropriately		
All kitchen floors and equipment are cleaned		
All dishes, utensils, and portioning equipment is washed, sanitized, air dried and positioned at work stations		
Fryers have been filtered and/or warm soaked and tested		

Products	Mgr Initials	
	PM	AM
Manager on duty completes and owns production guide		
Holding cabinet's temperature set as appropriate		
Low boy freezer stocked		
Drive thru area organized with all condiments		
Packing supplies and condiments stocked		
Production Charts are printed and posted		
Hot held products are available, prepped, portioned, and labeled with holding times		
Frozen ready-to-cook items are stocked and stored in the kitchen or cooks line freezer units for prompt accessibility		
Pre-cook products are in steam wells ready for portioning		

Comments

_____

_____

_____

_____

_____

_____

_____

_____

_____

_____

Rush ready

Day Manager:_____ Night Manager:_____

Mgr Initials

People	AM	PM
Staff properly deployed. Everyone knows primary and secondary position		
Drive thru service ambassadors only pull cars up if the car behind has food ready		
Opening manager communicates any special events expected		

Equipment	AM	PM
3 headsets in use and back up batteries charged		
All heating equipment working properly		
Cash drawers stocked with change/ Printers stocked with paper		
Condiments, paper goods, and utensils are stocked for projected sales volume in appropriate areas		
Lobby tables, floors, trash receptacles, windows , bathrooms, and condiment stand are clean, stocked and ready for guest use		
All trash cans have been emptied and cleaned appropriately		
All kitchen floors and equipment are cleaned		
All dishes, utensils, and portioning equipment is washed, sanitized, air dried and positioned at work stations		
Fryers have been filtered and/or warm soaked and tested		

Products	PM	AM
Mgr Initials		
Manager on duty completes and owns production guide		
Holding cabinet's temperature set as appropriate		
Low boy freezer stocked		
Drive thru area organized with all condiments		
Packing supplies and condiments stocked		
Production Charts are printed and posted		
Hot held products are available, prepped, portioned, and labeled with holding times		
Frozen ready-to-cook items are stocked and stored in the kitchen or cooks line freezer units for prompt accessibility		
Pre-cook products are in steam wells ready for portioning		

Comments

_____

_____

_____

_____

_____

_____

_____

_____

_____

_____

Rush ready

Day Manager:_____ Night Manager:_____

People	AM	PM
Staff properly deployed. Everyone knows primary and secondary position		
Drive thru service ambassadors only pull cars up if the car behind has food ready		
Opening manager communicates any special events expected		

Equipment	AM	PM
3 headsets in use and back up batteries charged		
All heating equipment working properly		
Cash drawers stocked with change/ Printers stocked with paper		
Condiments, paper goods, and utensils are stocked for projected sales volume in appropriate areas		
Lobby tables, floors, trash receptacles, windows , bathrooms, and condiment stand are clean, stocked and ready for guest use		
All trash cans have been emptied and cleaned appropriately		
All kitchen floors and equipment are cleaned		
All dishes, utensils, and portioning equipment is washed, sanitized, air dried and positioned at work stations		
Fryers have been filtered and/or warm soaked and tested		

Mgr Initials

Products	PM	AM
Manager on duty completes and owns production guide		
Holding cabinet's temperature set as appropriate		
Low boy freezer stocked		
Drive thru area organized with all condiments		
Packing supplies and condiments stocked		
Production Charts are printed and posted		
Hot held products are available, prepped, portioned, and labeled with holding times		
Frozen ready-to-cook items are stocked and stored in the kitchen or cooks line freezer units for prompt accessibility		
Pre-cook products are in steam wells ready for portioning		

Comments

_____

_____

_____

_____

_____

_____

_____

_____

_____

_____

Rush ready

Day Manager:_____   Night Manager:_____

Mgr Initials

People	AM	PM
Staff properly deployed. Everyone knows primary and secondary position		
Drive thru service ambassadors only pull cars up if the car behind has food ready		
Opening manager communicates any special events expected		

Equipment	AM	PM
3 headsets in use and back up batteries charged		
All heating equipment working properly		
Cash drawers stocked with change/ Printers stocked with paper		
Condiments, paper goods, and utensils are stocked for projected sales volume in appropriate areas		
Lobby tables, floors, trash receptacles, windows , bathrooms, and condiment stand are clean, stocked and ready for guest use		
All trash cans have been emptied and cleaned appropriately		
All kitchen floors and equipment are cleaned		
All dishes, utensils, and portioning equipment is washed, sanitized, air dried and positioned at work stations		
Fryers have been filtered and/or warm soaked and tested		

Mgr Initials

Products	PM	AM
Manager on duty completes and owns production guide		
Holding cabinet's temperature set as appropriate		
Low boy freezer stocked		
Drive thru area organized with all condiments		
Packing supplies and condiments stocked		
Production Charts are printed and posted		
Hot held products are available, prepped, portioned, and labeled with holding times		
Frozen ready-to-cook items are stocked and stored in the kitchen or cooks line freezer units for prompt accessibility		
Pre-cook products are in steam wells ready for portioning		

Comments

_____
_____
_____
_____
_____
_____
_____
_____
_____
_____

Rush ready

Day Manager:_____ Night Manager:_____

Mgr Initials

People	AM	PM
Staff properly deployed. Everyone knows primary and secondary position		
Drive thru service ambassadors only pull cars up if the car behind has food ready		
Opening manager communicates any special events expected		

Equipment	AM	PM
3 headsets in use and back up batteries charged		
All heating equipment working properly		
Cash drawers stocked with change/ Printers stocked with paper		
Condiments, paper goods, and utensils are stocked for projected sales volume in appropriate areas		
Lobby tables, floors, trash receptacles, windows , bathrooms, and condiment stand are clean, stocked and ready for guest use		
All trash cans have been emptied and cleaned appropriately		
All kitchen floors and equipment are cleaned		
All dishes, utensils, and portioning equipment is washed, sanitized, air dried and positioned at work stations		
Fryers have been filtered and/or warm soaked and tested		

Mgr Initials

Products	PM	AM
Manager on duty completes and owns production guide		
Holding cabinet's temperature set as appropriate		
Low boy freezer stocked		
Drive thru area organized with all condiments		
Packing supplies and condiments stocked		
Production Charts are printed and posted		
Hot held products are available, prepped, portioned, and labeled with holding times		
Frozen ready-to-cook items are stocked and stored in the kitchen or cooks line freezer units for prompt accessibility		
Pre-cook products are in steam wells ready for portioning		

Comments

_____

_____

_____

_____

_____

_____

_____

_____

_____

_____

Rush ready

Day Manager:_____ Night Manager:_____

People	AM	PM
Staff properly deployed. Everyone knows primary and secondary position		
Drive thru service ambassadors only pull cars up if the car behind has food ready		
Opening manager communicates any special events expected		
Equipment	**AM**	**PM**
3 headsets in use and back up batteries charged		
All heating equipment working properly		
Cash drawers stocked with change/ Printers stocked with paper		
Condiments, paper goods, and utensils are stocked for projected sales volume in appropriate areas		
Lobby tables, floors, trash receptacles, windows , bathrooms, and condiment stand are clean, stocked and ready for guest use		
All trash cans have been emptied and cleaned appropriately		
All kitchen floors and equipment are cleaned		
All dishes, utensils, and portioning equipment is washed, sanitized, air dried and positioned at work stations		
Fryers have been filtered and/or warm soaked and tested		

Products	Mgr Initials	
	PM	AM
Manager on duty completes and owns production guide		
Holding cabinet's temperature set as appropriate		
Low boy freezer stocked		
Drive thru area organized with all condiments		
Packing supplies and condiments stocked		
Production Charts are printed and posted		
Hot held products are available, prepped, portioned, and labeled with holding times		
Frozen ready-to-cook items are stocked and stored in the kitchen or cooks line freezer units for prompt accessibility		
Pre-cook products are in steam wells ready for portioning		

Comments

_____

_____

_____

_____

_____

_____

_____

_____

_____

Rush ready

Day Manager:_____ Night Manager:_____

Mgr Initials

People	AM	PM
Staff properly deployed. Everyone knows primary and secondary position		
Drive thru service ambassadors only pull cars up if the car behind has food ready		
Opening manager communicates any special events expected		

Equipment	AM	PM
3 headsets in use and back up batteries charged		
All heating equipment working properly		
Cash drawers stocked with change/ Printers stocked with paper		
Condiments, paper goods, and utensils are stocked for projected sales volume in appropriate areas		
Lobby tables, floors, trash receptacles, windows , bathrooms, and condiment stand are clean, stocked and ready for guest use		
All trash cans have been emptied and cleaned appropriately		
All kitchen floors and equipment are cleaned		
All dishes, utensils, and portioning equipment is washed, sanitized, air dried and positioned at work stations		
Fryers have been filtered and/or warm soaked and tested		

Products	Mgr Initials	
	PM	AM
Manager on duty completes and owns production guide		
Holding cabinet's temperature set as appropriate		
Low boy freezer stocked		
Drive thru area organized with all condiments		
Packing supplies and condiments stocked		
Production Charts are printed and posted		
Hot held products are available, prepped, portioned, and labeled with holding times		
Frozen ready-to-cook items are stocked and stored in the kitchen or cooks line freezer units for prompt accessibility		
Pre-cook products are in steam wells ready for portioning		

Comments

_____
_____
_____
_____
_____
_____
_____
_____
_____
_____

Rush ready

Day Manager:_____ Night Manager:_____

Mgr Initials

People	AM	PM
Staff properly deployed. Everyone knows primary and secondary position		
Drive thru service ambassadors only pull cars up if the car behind has food ready		
Opening manager communicates any special events expected		

Equipment	AM	PM
3 headsets in use and back up batteries charged		
All heating equipment working properly		
Cash drawers stocked with change/ Printers stocked with paper		
Condiments, paper goods, and utensils are stocked for projected sales volume in appropriate areas		
Lobby tables, floors, trash receptacles, windows , bathrooms, and condiment stand are clean, stocked and ready for guest use		
All trash cans have been emptied and cleaned appropriately		
All kitchen floors and equipment are cleaned		
All dishes, utensils, and portioning equipment is washed, sanitized, air dried and positioned at work stations		
Fryers have been filtered and/or warm soaked and tested		

Products	PM	AM
	Mgr Initials	
Manager on duty completes and owns production guide		
Holding cabinet's temperature set as appropriate		
Low boy freezer stocked		
Drive thru area organized with all condiments		
Packing supplies and condiments stocked		
Production Charts are printed and posted		
Hot held products are available, prepped, portioned, and labeled with holding times		
Frozen ready-to-cook items are stocked and stored in the kitchen or cooks line freezer units for prompt accessibility		
Pre-cook products are in steam wells ready for portioning		

Comments

_____

_____

_____

_____

_____

_____

_____

_____

_____

_____

Rush ready

Day Manager:_____ Night Manager:_____

People	AM	PM
Staff properly deployed. Everyone knows primary and secondary position		
Drive thru service ambassadors only pull cars up if the car behind has food ready		
Opening manager communicates any special events expected		
Equipment	**AM**	**PM**
3 headsets in use and back up batteries charged		
All heating equipment working properly		
Cash drawers stocked with change/ Printers stocked with paper		
Condiments, paper goods, and utensils are stocked for projected sales volume in appropriate areas		
Lobby tables, floors, trash receptacles, windows , bathrooms, and condiment stand are clean, stocked and ready for guest use		
All trash cans have been emptied and cleaned appropriately		
All kitchen floors and equipment are cleaned		
All dishes, utensils, and portioning equipment is washed, sanitized, air dried and positioned at work stations		
Fryers have been filtered and/or warm soaked and tested		

Products	PM	AM
Manager on duty completes and owns production guide		
Holding cabinet's temperature set as appropriate		
Low boy freezer stocked		
Drive thru area organized with all condiments		
Packing supplies and condiments stocked		
Production Charts are printed and posted		
Hot held products are available, prepped, portioned, and labeled with holding times		
Frozen ready-to-cook items are stocked and stored in the kitchen or cooks line freezer units for prompt accessibility		
Pre-cook products are in steam wells ready for portioning		

Mgr Initials

Comments

_____
_____
_____
_____
_____
_____
_____
_____
_____
_____

Rush ready

Day Manager:_____ Night Manager:_____

People	AM	PM
Staff properly deployed. Everyone knows primary and secondary position		
Drive thru service ambassadors only pull cars up if the car behind has food ready		
Opening manager communicates any special events expected		

Equipment	AM	PM
3 headsets in use and back up batteries charged		
All heating equipment working properly		
Cash drawers stocked with change/ Printers stocked with paper		
Condiments, paper goods, and utensils are stocked for projected sales volume in appropriate areas		
Lobby tables, floors, trash receptacles, windows , bathrooms, and condiment stand are clean, stocked and ready for guest use		
All trash cans have been emptied and cleaned appropriately		
All kitchen floors and equipment are cleaned		
All dishes, utensils, and portioning equipment is washed, sanitized, air dried and positioned at work stations		
Fryers have been filtered and/or warm soaked and tested		

Products	PM	AM
	Mgr Initials	
Manager on duty completes and owns production guide		
Holding cabinet's temperature set as appropriate		
Low boy freezer stocked		
Drive thru area organized with all condiments		
Packing supplies and condiments stocked		
Production Charts are printed and posted		
Hot held products are available, prepped, portioned, and labeled with holding times		
Frozen ready-to-cook items are stocked and stored in the kitchen or cooks line freezer units for prompt accessibility		
Pre-cook products are in steam wells ready for portioning		

Comments

_____
_____
_____
_____
_____
_____
_____
_____
_____
_____

Rush ready

Day Manager:_____ Night Manager:_____

Mgr Initials

People	AM	PM
Staff properly deployed. Everyone knows primary and secondary position		
Drive thru service ambassadors only pull cars up if the car behind has food ready		
Opening manager communicates any special events expected		

Equipment	AM	PM
3 headsets in use and back up batteries charged		
All heating equipment working properly		
Cash drawers stocked with change/ Printers stocked with paper		
Condiments, paper goods, and utensils are stocked for projected sales volume in appropriate areas		
Lobby tables, floors, trash receptacles, windows , bathrooms, and condiment stand are clean, stocked and ready for guest use		
All trash cans have been emptied and cleaned appropriately		
All kitchen floors and equipment are cleaned		
All dishes, utensils, and portioning equipment is washed, sanitized, air dried and positioned at work stations		
Fryers have been filtered and/or warm soaked and tested		

Products	Mgr Initials	
	PM	AM
Manager on duty completes and owns production guide		
Holding cabinet's temperature set as appropriate		
Low boy freezer stocked		
Drive thru area organized with all condiments		
Packing supplies and condiments stocked		
Production Charts are printed and posted		
Hot held products are available, prepped, portioned, and labeled with holding times		
Frozen ready-to-cook items are stocked and stored in the kitchen or cooks line freezer units for prompt accessibility		
Pre-cook products are in steam wells ready for portioning		

Comments

_____

_____

_____

_____

_____

_____

_____

_____

_____

_____

Rush ready

Day Manager:_____ Night Manager:_____

Mgr Initials

People	AM	PM
Staff properly deployed. Everyone knows primary and secondary position		
Drive thru service ambassadors only pull cars up if the car behind has food ready		
Opening manager communicates any special events expected		

Equipment	AM	PM
3 headsets in use and back up batteries charged		
All heating equipment working properly		
Cash drawers stocked with change/ Printers stocked with paper		
Condiments, paper goods, and utensils are stocked for projected sales volume in appropriate areas		
Lobby tables, floors, trash receptacles, windows , bathrooms, and condiment stand are clean, stocked and ready for guest use		
All trash cans have been emptied and cleaned appropriately		
All kitchen floors and equipment are cleaned		
All dishes, utensils, and portioning equipment is washed, sanitized, air dried and positioned at work stations		
Fryers have been filtered and/or warm soaked and tested		

Products	Mgr Initials	
	PM	AM
Manager on duty completes and owns production guide		
Holding cabinet's temperature set as appropriate		
Low boy freezer stocked		
Drive thru area organized with all condiments		
Packing supplies and condiments stocked		
Production Charts are printed and posted		
Hot held products are available, prepped, portioned, and labeled with holding times		
Frozen ready-to-cook items are stocked and stored in the kitchen or cooks line freezer units for prompt accessibility		
Pre-cook products are in steam wells ready for portioning		

Comments

_____
_____
_____
_____
_____
_____
_____
_____
_____
_____

Rush ready

Day Manager:_____ Night Manager:_____

Mgr Initials

People	AM	PM
Staff properly deployed. Everyone knows primary and secondary position		
Drive thru service ambassadors only pull cars up if the car behind has food ready		
Opening manager communicates any special events expected		

Equipment	AM	PM
3 headsets in use and back up batteries charged		
All heating equipment working properly		
Cash drawers stocked with change/ Printers stocked with paper		
Condiments, paper goods, and utensils are stocked for projected sales volume in appropriate areas		
Lobby tables, floors, trash receptacles, windows , bathrooms, and condiment stand are clean, stocked and ready for guest use		
All trash cans have been emptied and cleaned appropriately		
All kitchen floors and equipment are cleaned		
All dishes, utensils, and portioning equipment is washed, sanitized, air dried and positioned at work stations		
Fryers have been filtered and/or warm soaked and tested		

Mgr Initials

Products	PM	AM
Manager on duty completes and owns production guide		
Holding cabinet's temperature set as appropriate		
Low boy freezer stocked		
Drive thru area organized with all condiments		
Packing supplies and condiments stocked		
Production Charts are printed and posted		
Hot held products are available, prepped, portioned, and labeled with holding times		
Frozen ready-to-cook items are stocked and stored in the kitchen or cooks line freezer units for prompt accessibility		
Pre-cook products are in steam wells ready for portioning		

Comments

_____
_____
_____
_____
_____
_____
_____
_____
_____
_____

Rush ready

Day Manager:_____   Night Manager:_____

Mgr Initials

People	AM	PM
Staff properly deployed. Everyone knows primary and secondary position		
Drive thru service ambassadors only pull cars up if the car behind has food ready		
Opening manager communicates any special events expected		

Equipment	AM	PM
3 headsets in use and back up batteries charged		
All heating equipment working properly		
Cash drawers stocked with change/ Printers stocked with paper		
Condiments, paper goods, and utensils are stocked for projected sales volume in appropriate areas		
Lobby tables, floors, trash receptacles, windows , bathrooms, and condiment stand are clean, stocked and ready for guest use		
All trash cans have been emptied and cleaned appropriately		
All kitchen floors and equipment are cleaned		
All dishes, utensils, and portioning equipment is washed, sanitized, air dried and positioned at work stations		
Fryers have been filtered and/or warm soaked and tested		

Products	Mgr Initials	
	PM	AM
Manager on duty completes and owns production guide		
Holding cabinet's temperature set as appropriate		
Low boy freezer stocked		
Drive thru area organized with all condiments		
Packing supplies and condiments stocked		
Production Charts are printed and posted		
Hot held products are available, prepped, portioned, and labeled with holding times		
Frozen ready-to-cook items are stocked and stored in the kitchen or cooks line freezer units for prompt accessibility		
Pre-cook products are in steam wells ready for portioning		

Comments

_____

_____

_____

_____

_____

_____

_____

_____

_____

_____

Rush ready

Day Manager:_____   Night Manager:_____

People	AM	PM
Staff properly deployed. Everyone knows primary and secondary position		
Drive thru service ambassadors only pull cars up if the car behind has food ready		
Opening manager communicates any special events expected		

Equipment	AM	PM
3 headsets in use and back up batteries charged		
All heating equipment working properly		
Cash drawers stocked with change/ Printers stocked with paper		
Condiments, paper goods, and utensils are stocked for projected sales volume in appropriate areas		
Lobby tables, floors, trash receptacles, windows , bathrooms, and condiment stand are clean, stocked and ready for guest use		
All trash cans have been emptied and cleaned appropriately		
All kitchen floors and equipment are cleaned		
All dishes, utensils, and portioning equipment is washed, sanitized, air dried and positioned at work stations		
Fryers have been filtered and/or warm soaked and tested		

Products	Mgr Initials	
	PM	AM
Manager on duty completes and owns production guide		
Holding cabinet's temperature set as appropriate		
Low boy freezer stocked		
Drive thru area organized with all condiments		
Packing supplies and condiments stocked		
Production Charts are printed and posted		
Hot held products are available, prepped, portioned, and labeled with holding times		
Frozen ready-to-cook items are stocked and stored in the kitchen or cooks line freezer units for prompt accessibility		
Pre-cook products are in steam wells ready for portioning		

Comments

_____
_____
_____
_____
_____
_____
_____
_____
_____
_____

Rush ready

Day Manager:_____ Night Manager:_____

Mgr Initials

People	AM	PM
Staff properly deployed. Everyone knows primary and secondary position		
Drive thru service ambassadors only pull cars up if the car behind has food ready		
Opening manager communicates any special events expected		

Equipment	AM	PM
3 headsets in use and back up batteries charged		
All heating equipment working properly		
Cash drawers stocked with change/ Printers stocked with paper		
Condiments, paper goods, and utensils are stocked for projected sales volume in appropriate areas		
Lobby tables, floors, trash receptacles, windows , bathrooms, and condiment stand are clean, stocked and ready for guest use		
All trash cans have been emptied and cleaned appropriately		
All kitchen floors and equipment are cleaned		
All dishes, utensils, and portioning equipment is washed, sanitized, air dried and positioned at work stations		
Fryers have been filtered and/or warm soaked and tested		

Products	Mgr Initials	
	PM	AM
Manager on duty completes and owns production guide		
Holding cabinet's temperature set as appropriate		
Low boy freezer stocked		
Drive thru area organized with all condiments		
Packing supplies and condiments stocked		
Production Charts are printed and posted		
Hot held products are available, prepped, portioned, and labeled with holding times		
Frozen ready-to-cook items are stocked and stored in the kitchen or cooks line freezer units for prompt accessibility		
Pre-cook products are in steam wells ready for portioning		

Comments

_____
_____
_____
_____
_____
_____
_____
_____
_____
_____

Thank you for buying this book!

If you enjoyed this book, please leave a positive review on Amazon.com

If you didn't enjoy this book, please email me at rubyms@nmsu.edu and let me know why!

www.ingramcontent.com/pod-product-compliance
Lightning Source LLC
Chambersburg PA
CBHW051223170526
45166CB00005B/2015